BACKGAMMON OF TODAY

〜 BY 〜
JOHN LONGACRE

ILLUSTRATED
WITH DIAGRAMS SHOWING THE
BEST METHODS OF PLAY

BELL PUBLISHING COMPANY
NEW YORK

INTRODUCTION TO THE
1973 EDITION

The original "Today" of *Backgammon of Today* was 1930. With the current tremendous upsurge in the game's popularity Bell Publishing Company wanted to offer a top notch book on the subject and this book was recommended to the editors as truly outstanding. I was asked for my opinion of it and to do whatever updating or revisions I deemed necessary.

Well, in typical Fry fashion I proceeded to talk myself out of a nice fee. After reading the book with great pleasure and growing amazement I had to report to Bell's editors that "Today" holds good for 1973 as well as 1930 and the years between. And the foreseeable future for that matter. I found there was literally nothing I had to do to modernize the text. Mr. Longacre was way ahead of his time. I can honestly say that this book must improve your game and sadly say that Fry deserves none of the credit (unless these words have been instrumental in getting you to read it).

Part of the reason for Backgammon's renewed vitality is the introduction of the tournament circuit with its knockout matches, prize money, Calcutta pools etc. These competitions are taking place nowadays at glamour resorts all over the world at the rate of about one a month, and growing. They are fun and can be profitable too to a few. With some practice and this book you too can take a fling at the circuit and make a decent showing —at the worst you'll have had the fun of playing with the big boys. The *only difference* between tournament play and regular home or club games as covered in the pages to follow, is that you will have to make some slight adjustments in your offering and taking of doubles, depending on the running score of the particular match you are playing.

Make a few Primes today.

Sam Fry,
Games Editor, *Vogue* Magazine

FOREWORD

Backgammon is one of the oldest of games, and also one of the most widely played. Its origin is vaguely attributed to ancient Persia. Japan knew of it two thousand years ago. The Romans got it from Greek civilization and spread it over Europe. In India, it was the father of Parcheesi. The Aztecs played a recognizable variation of it before Cortez saw Mexico.

Consequently, a definitive treatise on all of the forms in which Backgammon is played today, throughout the world, would bulk like a volume of an encyclopaedia, and would probably be as little read.

The development and perfection of what may fairly be called—in this country, at least—the Backgammon of today, may be attributed to two New York clubs in which the game has been played intensively for over a generation. Here there has grown up a tradition of play which differs, in some respects, from the game as described in the one or two short treatises which are apparently the only authorities now available, but is exactly the game which, within the last two years, has attained such widespread popularity.

Nearly every game played today is a combination of luck and skill; and wherever the element of luck is present, it is apparently the modern usage to put a stake on the hazard of the game. Some games, indeed, derive their chief attraction from the accompanying stake. Others have such intrinsic interest in the test of adroitness and judgment necessarily involved in the competition that they need no such adventitious aid. Of these latter, Backgammon has always been a notable example.

Within recent years, however, some of its devotees, appreciating the present-day urge to inject a financial interest into everything, realized that this game —almost unique in the frequent shifts of fortune which mark its progress—was eminently adaptable to this modern requirement.

They thereupon evolved what is known as the "Doubling Game," providing a combination of elasticity in increase of the stake, so long as the issue is in doubt, with a possibility of self-protection when fortune is unfavorable, that is not found in any other game. This is probably the chief single factor in the present remarkable rejuvenation which is now taking place.

It is the purpose of this small book to describe the game as played with this variation, and to offer some suggestions for success thereat.

In making these suggestions, there has been a consistent effort to apply the test of mathematics in determining the comparative soundness, or desirability, of the various methods of play. It is

well to understand clearly the extent
to which reliance can be placed on this
standard.

When it is stated that the "mathematical odds" are 35-1 against, say,
double 4's, this does not mean that, in
thirty-six throws, double 4's will certainly
appear once, and only once. It simply
means that, if a pair of dice were thrown
to infinity, and *if* it were possible to stop
then, and reckon up, it would be found
that double 4's had been thrown a number of times exactly 1-36 of the total number of throws. Nothing more.

Therefore, general rules of play based on
mathematical probability are by no means
infallible guides, and exceptions to these
rules occur frequently. All that can be
said for them is, that in the long run
they should be found justified.

Acknowledgment is made of the per-
mission of the Town Crier of Philadel-
phia to republish matter originally ap-
pearing in their columns.

CONTENTS

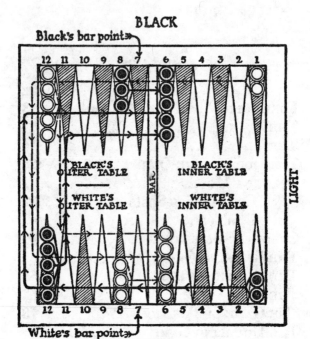

**BACKGAMMON BOARD SET UP FOR PLAY, SHOW-
ING DIRECTION OF MOVEMENT OF THE BLACK
AND WHITE MEN**

In this diagram and the other diagrams in the book, the
"tables" and "bar points" are indicated and each "point"
numbered. This is done in order to simplify explanation.
There are no such indications or numbers on a regular Backgammon Board.

THE BOARD

Backgammon is played on a specially designed rectangular board. Extending from the sides of the board nearest the players are twelve long triangles, or "points," alternately colored and pointing toward the center. A raised strip, or "bar," divides the board perpendicularly, so that each player has in front of him two sections, or "tables," of six points each.

Each player is provided with fifteen draughtsmen, or "men," white for one player, black for the other.

The men are set up in the board in the manner shown in the accompanying diagram. (See diagram 1.)

NOTE.—In all diagrams, the "tables" and "bar-points" are indicated and each "point" is numbered. This is in order to facilitate explanation. There are no such indications or numbers on a regular board.

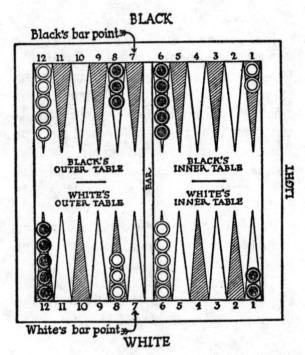

Diagram 1

THE BOARD

In former days, they played by the light of a candle, placed at one side of the board. Because of the raised "bar," the far "table" was imperfectly visible. It was necessary, then, that the important play should take place in the best-lighted side; therefore, down to the present day, the section nearest the light is the "inner table," the other side of the "bar" is the "outer table," and the board is arranged for play accordingly.

Here the light comes from the right; if it came from the left, the men would be shifted over, as in diagram 2.

The relative position of the men is not affected by this shift, but the direction of their movement is reversed. This does not change the method of play, in any way, but it is frequently confusing to the beginner; therefore it is well, at the start, to become accustomed to playing from either position.

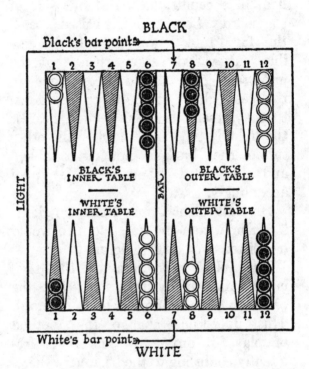

Diagram 2

THE BOARD

The actual position of the light, nowadays, is not a matter of importance, but occasionally a player distinctly prefers his inner table to be on one side rather than the other; in this case, the decision rests with the player throwing the higher single die.

THE PLAY

When the men are set up as in the diagram, each player casts a single die for the first move. He who throws the higher number wins, and plays the sum of the numbers, or "pips," on both his own and his opponent's die, by moving a man, or men, forward the number of points corresponding to the pips on the dice. After that, each player, in turn throws two dice and plays accordingly.

There is an alternative method for determining the first move. Each player throws two dice: the higher number wins, and may play his throw, but, if this is not a desirable combination, he may throw again. In this case, the second throw *must* be played, he has not the option of either throw.

The object of the game is to move the ten outside men into the inner table (five are already there) and then to remove the whole fifteen from the board (this is termed "throwing off" or "bearing") before the adversary can move and bear all his men in like manner.

The opponents move their men in opposite directions. (See diagram 3.)

Here, Black moves his men from left to right, like the hands of a clock; the two men on White's 1-point moving through White's inner table and outer table, Black's outer table, into his inner table, where they are thrown off. His five men on White's 12-point have only to cross his outer table, and the three on his 9-point merely move across the bar. White's men take a similar course, but from right to left. Progress must be continually toward the inner table, there is no moving backward.

Progress is determined by the number of pips thrown. For instance, if the throw is 5-4, one man may be moved forward nine points, or one man may move five and another four. It is always

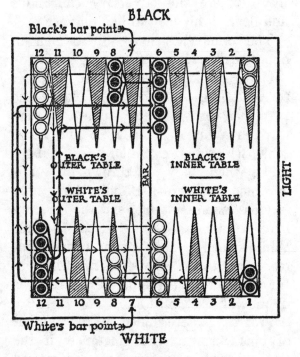

Diagram 3

optional to move any one of the men, but, in moving, a man may not rest on any point already occupied by two or more of the opponents. Therefore, with a throw of 5-4, it would not be possible to move one of the two men in the opponent's inner table forward five points for that would land him on the opponent's 6-point, which is already covered. The man could, however, be moved forward four points, and then five more, passing over the occupied 6-point and resting on the 10-point in the outer table.

It will be of assistance to the beginner to acquire the habit of thinking of his throw, not as a total, but as two distinct units. For instance, on throwing 4-3, the skilful player instinctively looks first for the best place to play a 4 and a 3; later, he considers the play of a 7.

While a man may not rest on a point occupied by two or more opponents, he may alight on a point held by only one. This is called "hitting" an opponent.

The vulnerable man, or "blot" as it is called, when so hit, no matter where he may be, is taken up and placed on the bar. A player whose man is on the bar, must "re-enter" this man before making any other move. "Re-entry" is to place a hit man on the board, in the inner table of the opponent, on a point indicated by he pips of the throw. (See diagram 4.)

Here, a Black man has been hit, and is on the bar. Black must re-enter in White's inner table, but White has been able, previously, to "make points," or, establish two men, on his 3 and 4, as well as holding his 6. Therefore, Black must throw either a 1, 2 or 5 to get in, since his man cannot rest on either the 3, 4 or 6. Should he throw, say 6-3, he cannot move any of his men, since he cannot re-enter the man on the bar. So White throws and plays, then Black throws again. Suppose he throws 4-2; the hit man is re-entered on the 2-point,

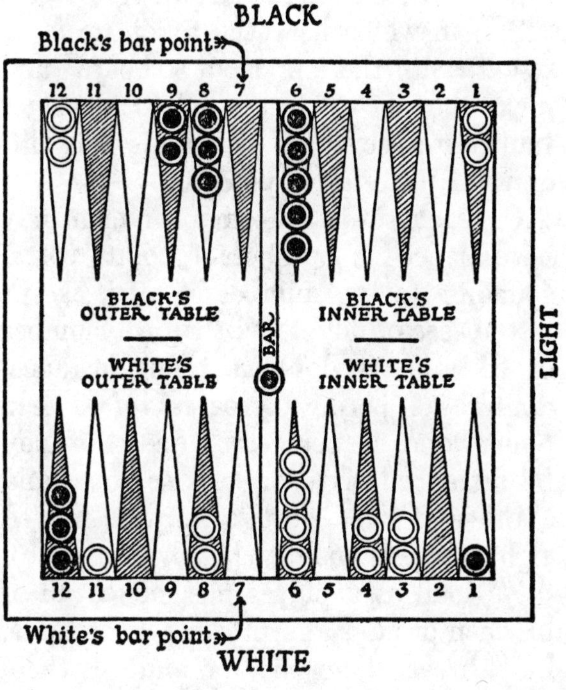

THE PLAY

BLACK

Black's bar point »

12 11 10 9 8 7 6 5 4 3 2 1

BLACK'S
OUTER TABLE

BLACK'S
INNER TABLE

BAR

WHITE'S
OUTER TABLE

WHITE'S
INNER TABLE

LIGHT

12 11 10 9 8 7 6 5 4 3 2 1

White's bar point »

WHITE

Diagram 4

and Black can use the 4 to move any other of his men, and the game proceeds.

A man which has been taken up must re-enter in the opponent's board and make the whole trip around to his inner table, irrespective of where he was hit, or what his original position.

On each throw, the man or men may be advanced a number of points corresponding to the number of pips, except in the case of doublets; then the number of the pips is doubled. For instance, double 4's permits progress of sixteen points, and, in using this, one man may be advanced sixteen; or one four, and another twelve; or two may be moved eight; or four may each move four.

As soon as a player has moved all of his men around and into his inner table, he "throws them off," or removes them from the board, according to the dice thrown, provided there are men on the points of the table corresponding to the pips thrown. If there are not, the men must be moved up in the board toward the 1-point. If the pips are in excess of the number required to move the farthest man to the 1-point, the man may be taken off. (See diagram 5.)

Here both sides have already thrown off some men. Black now throws 4-2. He has no men on either of these points, to take off; but he moves one man from his 6-point down two points to his 4, and he can now bear that man. White throws 6-4. He has nothing on his 6, but six is greater than five, therefore he takes one man from the 5-point. He has nothing on his 4-point, therefore he moves one man from the 5, four points down, to his 1-point.

Suppose Black's next throw is double 5's. He has only three men on that point, so he takes them off, and plays one man from the 6 down to his 1, for the fourth 5. Suppose White's next throw is double 1's. He has only one man on that point (moved down from

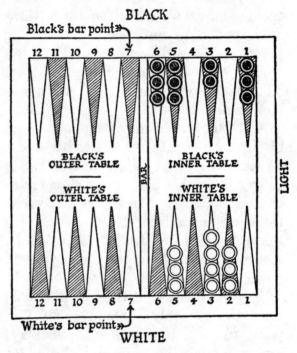

Diagram 5

the 5 on his previous throw), so he takes this off, moves a man on his 2 down one point to the 1 (that makes two of his four ones played), throws it off (three ones played), and moves one man on his 5 down to his 4-point, for the fourth one.

A player is not obliged to throw off a man, if either that man or another can be moved up the required number of points, but he must do one or the other.

Since the object of the game is to throw off the men as soon as possible, a man is never moved up, optionally, except as a measure of safety. (See diagram 6.)

Here White has thrown 4-2. He can take one man off the 2, and one off the 4, but that would be unwise because a single man would thereby be exposed on the 4-point. He can throw off one of the men on the 4 and move the other up two points, to his 2. But a careful player, realizing that the game is won, unless one of his men should be hit, would move up the two men on the 6, one to

BACKGAMMON OF TODAY

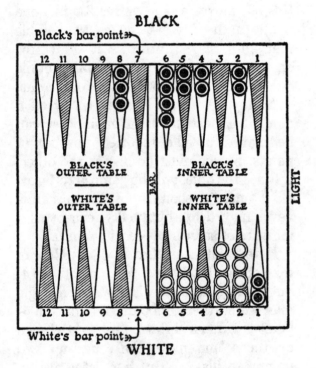

Diagram 6

the 4 and one to the 2, thereby materially decreasing the danger of a subsequent exposure.

The player first to throw off all of his
men wins a Single Game. If he has
thrown off *all* before his opponent has
thrown off *any*, he wins a Double Game,
or "Gammon." A Triple Game, or
"Backgammon," is won, if the player
has thrown off all his men before the
adversary has thrown off any man and
before all of the adversary's men have
been moved out of the winner's inner
table.

THE ODDS OF THE DICE

A cast of the dice is the proverbial synonym for uncertainty, and, in actual play, the frequent total disregard shown by the dice themselves for "mathematical odds" is one of the most delightful (or most exasperating) features of the game. Nevertheless, a complete familiarity with the mathematical probability of the occurrence of a single or combination number, when two dice are thrown, and an immediate perception of the relative values of these chances, are the basis of sound play. The habit, once acquired, of always weighing the odds when a choice of play presents itself, will save many a close game.

The computation is comparatively simple. For example: what is the chance of being hit, when a 2, exactly, must be thrown? The total number of different throws that can be made with two dice

THE ODDS OF THE DICE

is thirty-six. To hit a 2, the throw must be double-1, or double-2, or a 2 in combination with any of the other five numbers. Any combination shot may be thrown in two ways, but any doublet in only one. Therefore there are twelve shots which will hit, and twenty-four which will miss; and the odds are two to one against a hit.

Here is the complete table:

It is	25-11	or about	9-4	against	hitting	1
" "	24-12	"	2-1	"	"	2
" "	22-14	"	3-2	"	"	3
" "	21-15	"	7-5	"	"	4
" "	21-15	"	7-5	"	"	5
" "	19-17	"	9-8	"	"	6
" "	30-6	"	5-1	"	"	7
" "	30-6	"	5-1	"	"	8
" "	31-5	"	6-1	"	"	9
" "	33-3	"	11-1	"	"	10
" "	34-2	"	17-1	"	"	11
" "	33-3	"	11-1	"	"	12
" "	35-1	"		"	"	15, 16, 18, or 20

These are the odds *with all points open,* but they may be changed materially in actual play. For instance: (See diagram 7.)

Here Black has thrown 6-3. The game is probably lost if he cannot save the outside lone man. It cannot be left where it is, exposed to two direct shots and one combination; and it cannot be brought home, since White occupies the 5-point. Shall he move to his 11 or his 8? On the 11, White must throw a 6 to hit. The odds against a 6 (as shown above) are 9-8, nearly an even chance, but not against *this* 6, because neither 5-1 nor 4-2 will play. White must throw either double-3, double-6 or a combination 6, twelve possible shots out of thirty-six, and the odds here are 2-1 against. On the 8, White must throw a 3, against which the odds (above) are 3-2. But again, not against *this* 3, for double-1 and 2-1 will not play. He must throw either double-3 or a combination 3, eleven out

THE ODDS OF THE DICE

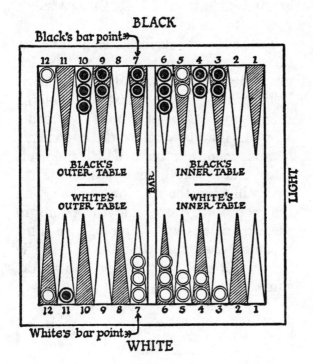

Diagram 7

of thirty-six, or 9-4 against. This is greater odds than 2-1, so Black's safest play is to his 8.

The chances against being hit are, however, only a part of the odds which must be borne in mind during play. When a man is hit, he must be re-entered before any other play may be made. Early in the play, before the opponent's board is made up, this is of little moment, since double-6 is the only possible throw that will keep the man on the bar. As the game progresses, and the points in the board fill up, a prompt re-entry becomes vital, since the loss of a single throw will often decide the fate of the game.

Here are the odds about re-entering:

With 5 points open,	35-1 on
" 4 " "	8-1 "
" 3 " "	3-1 "
" 2 " "	5-4 against
" 1 point "	9-4 "

THE ODDS OF THE DICE

In this game, the dice will frequently vary widely from the mathematical expectation; nevertheless, sound play must be based on the law of averages, therefore the beginner will do well to acquire complete familiarity with the tables given above, and to accustom himself to readily adapt them to the situations of actual play.

OPENING MOVES

A—Combination Shots

It is possible to play any of the opening throws of combination shots in half a dozen different ways, but, to obtain the maximum advantage, the choice is narrowly limited. For some throws, the difference of opinion on the relative merit of safety and boldness offers two or three alternatives; for others, sound play indicates only one method of execution.

The order of precedence given below for alternative play indicates simply an individual opinion. In the conduct of the game, good reasons can be adduced for both caution and boldness, and it would be presumptuous to assert the positive superiority of either course. It is only certain that, whatever may be the tactics adopted, they will often be discredited by the subsequent development, thus, at least, affording satisfaction to the critical onlookers.

Play one man from opponent's 1-point to join the five men on his 12-point.

Two-thirds of the journey is thus safely accomplished.

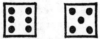

(a) One man from opponent's 12 to the bar point, the other from opponent's 1 to his 5.

This is a good example of a gamble for position. It is almost an even chance that the man on the bar point will be hit. Nevertheless, if it is hit, the odds are 7-5 that a point can be established on the opponent's 5 either by the enterer or by the man on the 1. This is one of the important strategical points, and amply compensates for the delay in progress caused by the hit. If the man on the bar is not hit, it is 5-2 that on the next shot the man can either be covered or used to make a valuable point. As for the man on the opponent's 5, it is 6-1 that the opponent will not be able to hit him and make a point. It would be very poor play to hit the man and leave a blot.

(b) One man from opponent's 1 to 11.

Here it is not entirely safe, since it can be hit by a 2; but this is a 9-4 chance against, since the opponent's throw of double-1 is blocked. If unhit, good progress has been made.

(c) Make the 2-point.

This is the only completely safe way to play the shot, but it has the great disadvantage of putting two men out of play immediately and permanently.

(d) One man to the bar; one to the 9.

Undesirable—too risky. It is 3-2 that one of the blots will be hit, in which case the odds are against the probability of both entering the hit man and pointing with the remaining blot, on the next throw.

(a) One man to the bar point; one man to opponent's 4.

This is not so attractive as the first alternative under 6-4, because the opponent's 4-point is no so desirable as his 5, but it is the most constructive use of the shot.

(b) One man from opponent's 1 to his 10.

Less ground is lost, if hit.

(c) One man to the bar; one to the 10.

Undesirable. See 6-4 (d) above. It is 19-17 that one man, and 1-11 that both men, will be hit. If hit, the odds are against a satisfactory succeeding shot.

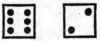

(a) One man to the bar, one man to the 11.

Again, there is a nearly even chance that the man on the bar will be hit, and a further chance of 1-17 that both blots will be hit, But if not hit, it is nearly 3-1 that the bar point can be made on the next throw.

(b) One man to the 5.

This is not quite so good as (a) because, while
the chances of being hit are less (3-2 as against
9-8) the probability of making the point if
not hit is only 7-5 as against 3-1.

(c) One man to opponent's 9.

Poor. The blot is just as vulnerable as in (b),
(because in one case double-1 couldn't be
used, and in the other, it shouldn't be used,
to make the hit) and an escape gives no
advantage in position. The only thing to
be said for this alternative is that, if hit, less
ground is lost.

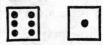

Make the bar-point by playing one
from 8 and one from opponent's 12.

One of the best of possible throws.

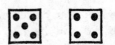

**(a) One from opponent's 12 to the 8;
the other from opponent's 1 to his 5.**

(*b*) Two from opponent's 12; one to the 8 and one to the 9.

This provides a useful builder and is not an especially vulnerable blot.

(*c*) Run with one man from opponent's 1 to his 10.

This gains full distance, but is vulnerable, and has no great outlook for position.

 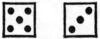

(*a*) Two men from opponent's 12, one to the 8, one to the 10.

This provides builders, and keeps the men in play.

(*b*) Make the 3-point.

An isolated point, deep in the board, so early in the game, is not of sufficient immediate value to warrant putting two men out of play. Of course, the point steadily increases in value as the game progresses, but now the play is premature.

(c) One man from opponent's **12 to the 5.**

The same play as 6-2 *(b).* Not attractive here since the shot can be played usefully without so much risk.

(a) One man to the 8; the other to the 11.

Builders. It is just as well to get an extra man on the 8 early, these men are most useful in making points in the board, and may be needed at any time. Moreover, with only the original three men, double-1 strips this point to an uncomfortable blot.

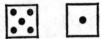

(a) One man to the 8; the other to the 5.

This is the same situation which was discussed under alternative 6-2 *b.*

(b) One man to the 8; the other to opponent's 2.

Safe, but nothing more.

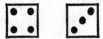

(a) One man to the 10, the other to the 9.

Providing two excellent builders, with about 4-1 against either being hit.

(b) One man to the 10, the other to opponent's 5.

One builder, and a move toward a strategic point.

(c) One to the 9, one to opponent's 4.

Not so good, because each of these blots is slightly easier to hit, while the possible resulting advantage, if they are not hit, is not so great.

(d) One man to opponent's 5, the other to his 4.

Would be a bad play, because this would allow the adversary to solve uncomfortable shots by moving unprotected men up in his board, beyond the two men just played. The nuisance value of one man held back on the 1-point is considerable; it delays the adversary's free progress more than any point that can be made.

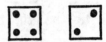

(*a*) Make the 4-point.

No alternative.

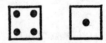

(*a*) One man to the 5, one to the 9.

A good gamble; it is 5-4 against either, and 8-1 against both, being hit, and 5-1 that the 5-point will be made, if they escape.

(*b*) One man to the 5; one to opponent's 5

3-2 against hitting the blot in the board. Not so much support if not hit—2-1 that the man can be covered. If hit, it is 7-5 that the opponent's 5-point can be made.

(*c*) One man to the 9, the other to opponent's 2.

Safer, and provides a builder.

(*d*) One man to the 8.

Ultraconservative.

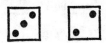

(*a*) One man to the 11, the other to the 10.

Provides two advantageous builders, with better than 6-1 against either being hit.

(*b*) One to the 11, one to opponent's 3.

A builder and a move toward a point. Not so good.

(*c*) One to the 8.

Safe, but a waste of the shot.

(*d*) To start both men in the adversary's board would be bad play; see 4-3 *d*.

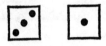

Make the 5-point.

Ranked with 6-1 as one of the best possible openers.

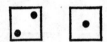

(*a*) One to the 11, the other to the 5.

A good risk. The opponent has a 5-7 chance to hit the blot on the 5, and a 1-17 chance to hit both men with a 6-4. But, if not hit, it is 4-1 that the next shot will cover the 5.

(*b*) One man to the 10.

Safer and provides a builder.

OPENING MOVES

B—Doublets

In general desirability, all doublets rank above any of the combination shots except 6-1 and 3-1. When the board is open, they are all favorable, as they are the only method by which a point of two men can be moved intact, and the fact that the number on the pips is doubled allows the maximum distance to be covered. This is the order of their relative value:

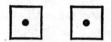

Is the best possible throw, because at one stroke is established the two most important points—the 5 in the inner table and the bar-point.

With such a start it may be possible, in a few throws, to block the escape of the opponent from the inner table. While this does not assure a win, it is an overwhelming advantage.

It is a common saying, that this throw cannot be played *dis*-advantageously.

(*a*) Two men to the 9, two to the opponent's 5.

(*b*) Two men from opponent's 12 to make the 5-point.

Of the first two alternatives (*a*) seems distinctly best, in spite of the undeniable advantage of the 5-point, because with two useful builders, this point may soon be made, and the prompt nullification of a successful adverse block, by occupying the opponent's 5, is a lasting advantage.

(*c*) Make the 4- and 2-points.

Three established points reduce the opponent's chance to re-enter, if hit; but the odds are still 3-1 on immediate entry, therefore this play does not seem warranted except as a *second* shot, when one of the adverse men in the inner table has been exposed and can be hit.

(a) Two men to the bar, and two to the opposing bar.

> Affords the maximum of progress, and an enormous lead in the race has been gained. No alternative.
>
> It may be well here to consider, parenthetically, the alternatives for this throw, when a *second* shot, and when the opponent has been able to make his bar-point. In this case, the advantage of this throw is materially lessened. The two men in the adverse table cannot move, therefore;

(a) Four men to the bar.

> This has the great disadvantage of leaving only a blot on the opposing 12-point, which is the only safety spot for the rear men on the trip around. But the whole distance is gained where it is needed, and there is now a good possibility of blocking in the two opposing men in the inner table. It is a close question, but the desertion of the three back men would seem justified, since no block has yet

been formed against them, and one or two hits could be sustained without losing the lead.

(*b*) Three men to the bar, and one from the 8 to the 2.

This maintains the valuable midway point, and puts only one man out of action. Of course, there is a 4-9 chance that this blot will be hit.

(*c*) Two men to the bar and two men to the 2-point.

Is not good; two men are permanently out of service, and the value of this point is negligible until late in the game.

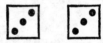

(*a*) Two men to the 5, two to the opponent's 4.

(*b*) Make the bar-point.

(*c*) Make both the 5- and 3-points in the table.

Is hardly desirable. One of these points is good, but the other alternatives use this throw to better advantage.

As a *second* shot the choice between (*a*) and (*b*) is very even, provided the adverse point in the inner table has not been broken; but, if the two men are separated in the inner table, (*a*) leaves a blot on the 8 which will be easy to hit; therefore (*b*), which is safe, is preferable.

Is advantageously available for fewer men than any other doublet, but it is a great help in progress.

(*a*) Two men from opponent's 12 to make the 3-point.

No alternative.

(*a*) The 5-point in the adverse table.

Is best.

(*b*) Make the 4-point and the opposing 3-point.

This latter provides a fairly reliable defense against a block.

(*c*) Make the 10- and 4-points.

Third choice.

OPENING STRATEGY

Since the object of each player is to be the first to carry his men to his inner table and throw them off, it follows that the primary strategy is twofold: to make all speed for home, and to delay the progress of the opponent. Sometimes the right course is indicated immediately, but often definite action cannot be soundly taken until after several throws.

The strategy of Backgammon is much like that of a war game where the contending forces are of equal strength, occupy equally advantageous positions, and are in plain view of each other. To complete the analogy, each side should possess the same speed and freedom of movement, but in Backgammon this factor is governed by the dice, and it is just here that the alertness and ready adaptability to constantly changing conditions—which are the qualifications of a good Backgammon player—are demonstrated. If the dice are favorable, the very most must be made of an advantage which may be only temporary; if unfavorable, the best defense must be immediately put into execution. If Fortune hesitates between the two forces, the army, which is necessarily all the time in motion, must be kept in balance, ready either for attack or defense, when the right moment comes, and not committed prematurely, and possibly irrevocably, to the wrong course. It is in this period of early maneuvering, before either side has a decided advantage in the dice, that the skilful player will build up a winning position before his less experienced opponent realizes it.

Strategy begins as soon as the men have begun to move. The relative position varies with each throw, and success follows the ability to correctly appraise the situation at any time, to decide which line of action has most promise of victory, and to select and execute the proper plays.

Frequently a beginner, as the game goes against him, and he fails to throw the "miracle shots" necessary for success, will rail at his bad luck. In the great majority of cases, the real explanation of his plight will be found in his failure to use good judgment in his earlier moves.

There are several major tactics, offensive and defensive, excellent individually, which may contribute to the victory; but if their execution be premature, or delayed too long, or made at too great expense of the available resources, or be not harmonious with the general plan, they may be directly responsible for the loss of the game.

Faulty co-ordination is generally the chief mistake of the beginner. He will make a play, otherwise commendable, just when it has no place in, or is directly counter to, the indicated strategy of the moment. The furthermost men are speeded home when the opponent is far ahead; a block is made after the adversaries have gone; points are made in the board when the outside men should be speeded, or vice versa. Once a style of play is adopted, no moves should be made except such as will directly further the success of that line of action.

If the early throws show little advantage to either side it is best to maintain a balanced game, as far as possible, until a definite course is indicated. There should be no haste in starting forward both men on the opponent's 1-point; one man retained on that point makes much more difficult the construction of the adverse board. Men should not be moved far back in the inner table, early in the game, even to make points; this reduces the forces available for maneuver, and is one of the most difficult handicaps to overcome.

OPENING STRATEGY

Broadly speaking, the game should be developed into one of four distinct styles of play: (1) The Running Game; (2) The Blocking Game; (3) The Back Game; (4) The Game of Position. The selection of the particular strategy to be followed, however, lies with the dice, rather than with the player. That is, the first few throws may so strongly indicate the best course as to elminate independent choice. Extraordinary initial long shots practically force a Running Game, which is the least desirable form of attack. Especially favorable throws will make possible a Blocking Game, which has the best promise of victory. Immediate, overwhelming advantage in progress by the opponent necessitates a Back Game, the most difficult of all, but, under the circumstances, the only chance of successful defense. The absence of the throws which definitely call for one or the other of these three plans, permits the Game of Position, which is the most evenly balanced of the four, and which may be said to be the use of normal throws to obtain the best position from which to press home an advantage, as and when the opportunity offers.

THE RUNNING GAME

A running game, in which everything is subordinated to speed in progress, would (win with only a slight superiority in throwing, provided none of the men were hit. But this is hard to avoid, and since, when a man is hit, it requires three average throws (25 pips) to re-enter, carry around and throw him off, it is clear that one or two hits will go far to offset a great superiority in high throws. Moreover, such a game offers the minimum of opposition to the progress of the adversary, and, if it is once slowed up, recovery of the lead is pure luck, since the position offers little hope of a successful defense.

It is, as has been said, the least desirable form of attack, but, with two or three exceptionally large throws at the start, it would be folly not to turn this handicap to the best advantage.

Once the men are well on their way, the chief care should be to provide for their safe arrival. Points in the board are now most necessary, particularly as the adversary will be in no hurry to move out of the inner table. If the adverse point on the 1 has already been broken, so much the better. Every chance should be taken to make points in the board beyond the adverse men. A blot in the board should not be hit, if, in re-entering, the man might be able to join his companion to make a lower point.'

No effort should be made to block the adversary; to hit an adverse blot would add to the difficulty of safe homecoming, with a quite incommensurate advantage in the delay of the opponent. The initial advantage in progress should be enough to win.

If the inner table is clear of opponents, no throw should be spent in improving the position in the board of men already

THE RUNNING GAME

home, unless the throw would cause a blot, if played by the outside men.

If a blot must be left, try to arrange the exposure against a combination shot (one needing two dice) only. If this is impossible, place the exposure as near as may be to the threatening opponent. It is harder to throw a 1 than, say, a 4.

If there is a choice of exposures, risk the man furthest from home. Less progress has been lost if it is hit.

THE BLOCKING GAME

A well-established blocking game is an almost certain winner, with a good prospect of a double game. As its name implies, the purpose of this strategy is to prevent the escape of the adversaries in the inner table. Unusually good throws, like double-1, double-4, etc., are generally necessary, for the effective points must be made promptly, since an alert adversary will make every effort to escape from the impending trap at once.

Builders are brought into the outer table as soon as possible, neglecting the advancement of the furthermost men; and rightly, for these may be brought around at leisure, once the block is in force.

A consecutive sequence of six points (known as a "side prime") is, of course, impassable, and is effective anywhere. It is generally grouped from the 10 to

the 5, or from the 9 to the 4, inclusive.
Once formed, it is not difficult to work
it steadily into the inner table.

If the "side prime" cannot be made
complete, it is better to arrange points
to block the moves of a 5 or 6 by the
prisoners, leaving any open spaces near
them. Thus, escape can only be effected
by a combination shot.

If the imprisoned adversaries do not
form a point, it is well to bring loose men
across the "side prime" to hit the blots
as soon as possible. The "prime,"
itself, should never be broken, except to
be immediately reformed further on. (See
diagram 8.)

Here, White should utilize a 5 to hit
the blot on the 4-point. It matters
nothing if Black hits this blot on re-
entry, because it is simply entered and
brought around again—and the two opponents are still trapped. If Black does
not throw a 4, White uses the next 6
he throws to move from 10 to 4, covering

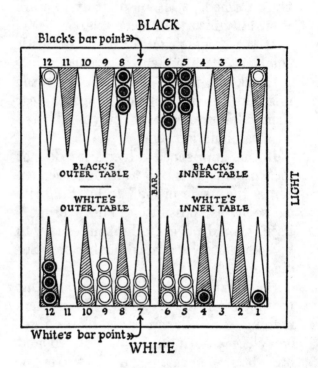

Diagram 8

his blot, and moving the "prime" one point further into the board.

Suppose, in the position illustrated, that White threw 6-4. It would be bad play to hit the blot and make a point by playing one man each from the 10 and 8, because that breaks the "prime," and Black, throwing 5-3, would re-enter and get nearly free, hitting the white blot at the same time.

The object of hitting the imprisoned blots, and working the "prime" into the inner table as soon as possible, is, by delaying Black's re-entry, to prevent him from getting all his other outside men home before White begins to throw off. If, at that time, Black has more men than the two prisoners to get home, the possibility of a double game for White is by that much increased.

THE BACK GAME

This is at once the most interesting and the most difficult strategy in the game. Moreover, it is a fight against odds, for a winning back game wins singly, but a losing back game often loses doubly. It can be justified only when the opponent has gained such an initial advantage in progress that the prospect of successful competition in a forward game is hopeless. But, in such a position, it offers the only chance of success, it is extremely hard to defeat, if well established, and it is the most satisfactory of victories.

The strategy of the back game is to establish a number of men on the lower points in the adversary's board so that there will come a time, when he is throwing off, when he must leave a blot which can be hit. Then the men of the back-player work forward toward their home table, spread out in open order to make sure, first, of continually hitting the re-entered man on his lonely trip home, and also, of gradually making the points which will block him in. As this block becomes effective, the points held in the opposing board are stripped to one man, in order to permit the opponent to play his small throws, thereby exposing further blots. These if hit, and perforce entered behind the newly formed block, are helpless to escape before their jailers, in turn, are being thrown off. Then the several shots necessary to bring them back home give time for the back-player to bear his men off with every shot, and an apparently insuperable lead is thus overcome. (See diagram 9.)

In this position, Black is 160 pips, say twenty throws, better than White, in progress. Suppose, however, Black throws 5-2, and White hits the consequent unavoidable blot. White has an excellent chance to win, because he has

BACKGAMMON OF TODAY

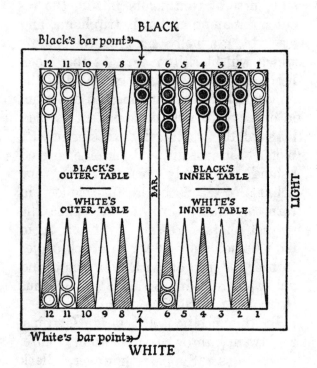

Diagram 9

timed his game so as to keep his men in play until they are needed. Diagram 10 shows the back game in a later stage:

Here Black has already borne seven men, but suppose he throws 5-4, and White hits both blots. White can bring his men home before the re-entered men can get away. It would take six average throws to bring the two Black men around, and by that time, White, throwing off meanwhile, should be well ahead.

In both the above instances it has been assumed that the player apparently in the lead has made a singularly unlucky throw. The point to be noted, however, is, that the back-player was able to turn an apparent defeat into a probable victory because he had timed the previous movements of his men so as to have them in the most effective position at the important moment.

Correct timing is an absolute essential. Even if the forward player is well ahead, he will take a number of throws

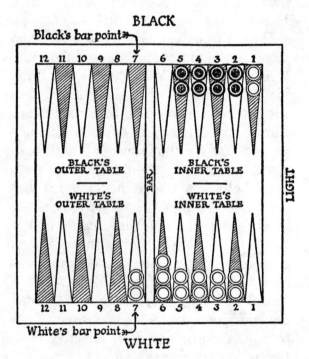

Diagram 10

before he is forced into the vulnerable position of Black, in Diagram 9. All this time, the back-player is throwing as well, and his men must keep moving, accordingly, until his chance comes. Unless he has had this in mind, and has allowed for it by slowing his men up, from the beginning of his back game, his men will have been compelled to run ahead of their schedule, and he finds himself in a position like this: (See diagram 11.)

Here Black is in the position of the first illustration, but now, even if he throws the unlucky 5-2 and White hits the blot, White has no board to effectually stop re-entry and no force of sharpshooters to bring down the returning opponent, and Black should win the game easily.

Therefore, once you have determined on a back game, you must slow up your progress immediately. You cannot expect the dice to help you in this—6's

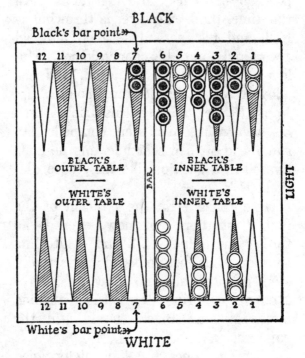

Diagram 11

and 5's are just as apt to be thrown as 1's and 2's. Extraordinary steps are necessary. You *must* have a number of men in the opponent's inner table— the more, the better, in fact, provided you can occupy the desirable points. The only way to get the men back there is to have them hit, and naturally, an alert opponent will not play your game for you, but will avoid your blots even to the point of leaving blots himself. So you must scatter your men so that he can not avoid hitting them, and, if you take him, make blots in your board which he must hit on re-entry—but be careful not to make the blots deep in the board, for they will be avoided by the re-enterer, and be prematurely out of play.

The blots laid for a back game should be made by men from the 6-point in the inner table, if possible; if not, by men from the 8, rather than by men from the opponent's 12. The maximum distance is thus lost, and the necessary slowing-up is more effectually accomplished. The blots in the board of the forward player will only be exposed late in the game, therefore the progress of the back-playing men must have been so slow as to permit them, at that time, to cover the outer tables so effectually as to constantly hit, and repeatedly drive back, the forward man, when it is re-entered. If too many of the back-playing men are already home, there will not be a large enough force to check the re-entered man's return.

Avoid making points in your board early; if you have hit an opponent, a point may delay him—which is just what you do not want to do until later in the game. An early blocking game may well be combined with a forward game —never with a back game.

In re-entering your men in the adversary's board, try first to occupy the 1- and 2-points, then either the 4- or the 5-. If you can make these three, you have started well. If you cannot make *either* the 1 or the 2, give up the idea—a back game is hopeless. The 4 or 5 is desirable, because the opponent can so easily maintain a block on the small points. This forces you to use your long shots on your outside men, and brings them prematurely into your own board, and out of useful play.

If you can make, say, the 1, 2 and 5, then the more men you can contrive to have hit, the better, since they have a stepping-stone to jump any block, and the disadvantage of untimely long shots is minimized since you can use them to work out the surplus men on the small points. Three points are not absolutely necessary however: a back game may well be successful with only the 1 and 2, or even the 1 and 3, if the outside men are well placed.

If you have succeeded in taking a blot which he has been compelled to make,

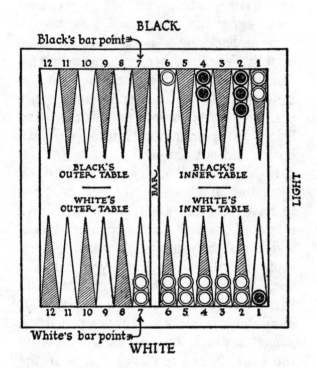

Diagram 12

in throwing off, give him every opportunity to make another. For instance, in this position: (See diagram 12.)

Take the first opportunity to break the point in the opponent's board, enabling him to play a 3, which he could not do otherwise, and possibly to leave you another blot.

If you can get another of his men on the Bar, you should win the game. You then will have two of his men blocked in on your 1-point until you are ready to throw off. It should take six average shots to bring these two men into his inner table, and he will then have seven men still to bear. With your corresponding six shots you will be unlucky if you have not more than caught up with him.

But note, also, that if you do not hit another man, but simply bring your outside men around and bear them off, you should lose, since his one man can get home in three throws, and you can only expect to have borne off six men, leaving nine, when he starts again to throw off his six.

Back play, to win, must be started early in the game. The fact that several of your men have been hit does not put you in position to play back with any chance of success *if your outside men are too far advanced.* If they are already well around, a situation generally develops where either you are crowded far into your board, and must relinquish the higher points, or you must prematurely break the points in the opponent's board. Then it becomes a question, not of winning, but of saving a double game.

———

The defense to a back game consists, first, in prevention. The adversary must have men on the Bar to carry out this strategy. A hit man undoubtedly hinders the opponent's progress, but this can easily be overdone. One of the commonest faults of the beginner is to conscien-

tiously hit every blot that is exposed.
Avoid having more than three opponents
on the bar or in your board, unless you
already have some points made or have
brought up useful builders with which
to point when hitting a re-enterer. Be
careful of this until the adverse game is
so far developed that back-play would
be out of timing.

Suppose, however, that a back game
has been well established against you.
Then do not be in a hurry to get home.
Try to establish points in your outer
board which will block the opponent
from using his inconvenient long throws
to move out his surplus men. (See diagram 13.)

Suppose, in this position, Black throws
6-3. It would be very bad play to make
a point on the 10, and move the blot on
the 9 to safety into his board. He
should make his bar-point, leaving blots
on White's 9 and 12. Long shots would
then compel the adversary to crowd up

BACKGAMMON OF TODAY

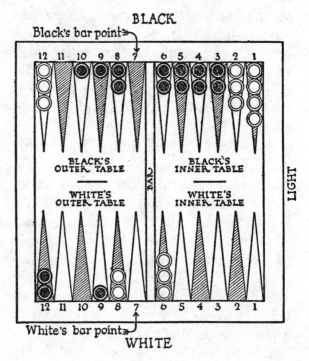

Diagram 13

his outside men, since those on the 1
and 2 points in Black's board cannot
move. Furthermore, if one of these blots
is hit, Black's game is improved, since
he has just so much longer to maneuver
without detriment, while each corresponding throw is crowding the opponent
more and more out of position.

THE GAME OF POSITION

If definite action has not been immediately forced by the unusual throws of either side, the opportunity is given for a game of position, which is really a balanced development of both offensive and defensive, as distinguished from the specialized offence either by superior speed or by intensive blockade, and the forced defence against overwhelming superiority in progress.

The tactics here consist in first securing the really important points, and then developing a game combining progress with effective hindrance of the adversary.

The outstanding desirable points are: the bar, the 5, and the opponent's 5. It is a close choice between the two first. If the two opposing men are still in the inner table—more especially, if their point has not been broken, the bar is most desirable, because it is the keystone of a blockade which is still quite possible. If one, or both, of the opponents have gotten away, or, perhaps, even if they are separated in the inner table, the 5 becomes most important, since, beside being a necessary part of any block, it, next to the 6, which is already held, is the most useful point to close against adverse re-entry, and its establishment cuts these odds immediately from 35-1 to 8-1. The bar, of course, is no hindrance to re-entry.

The establishment of the 5-point in the opponent's table precludes any effective block on his part and affords a sure base for re-entry at the point of easiest departure. With this assured, the outside men may be advanced more boldly. Furthermore, this point threatens any blot in his outside table.

Without the aid of lucky dice, these vantage points are gained only by risking blots which, if hit, involve definite, and possibly serious loss of progress. Nevertheless, a strong position is worth a considerable risk. Some of the alternatives given for the opening throws are illustrative of these tactics. The loss of men in this cause is nowhere nearly so expensive when the adverse table is still open. The real damage from a hit comes when the opponent gains a throw, or, maybe, two, by having established points which delay re-entry; a lost throw is a severe handicap to overcome. Therefore it is essential that such risks be taken as early in the game as possible.

Just how far sacrifices for position should be carried, depends a good deal on the corresponding position of the adversary, but a certain amount of persistence would seem to be justified. Occasionally, every blot is unerringly hit; but if, as often happens, there then ensues a rapid alternating replacement of two or three men, with no improvement in the opponent's board, the situation is not necessarily serious—possibly far from it. Four or five men in the opponent's inner table are an enormous increase in the available mobile force,— and at the point of greatest efficiency. It is certain that the progress of the adverse men will be much more than usually difficult with such an increased force opposed to them, and an early disparity in mere distance covered is frequently evened by a few lucky throws.

It may be noted here, parenthetically, that a situation where several men have been hit, but the adversary *has made little advance in progress,* is not such as to call for a back game. (See diagram 14.)

Here Black is about eight throws ahead in progress, but *only by comparison;* his men have made little actual advance. He has no position, and, without exceptionally lucky throws, will expose several blots to White's oncoming men. White's game is excellently placed to follow up any advantage, and he may well win.

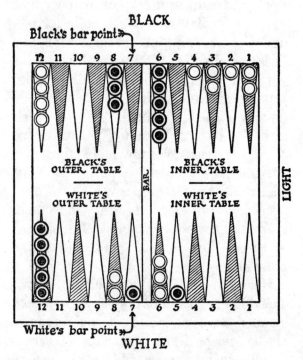

Diagram 14

Moreover, at this point, because of his slight progress, Black could easily slow up and make a block in his outer board which would throw a back game out of timing.

The 5 is the only point in the board worth the exposure of a blot. In fact, for this style of development, the lower points, if isolated, are initially a disadvantage, since they put men out of play too early. Of course, if joined to the outer points, they are excellent, but this possibility is remote. Points in the outer board can be linked up into a completely effective blockade, and, at the same time, serve as valuable stepping stones to safety for the rear men. Therefore builders in the outer board are very desirable, and a blot here can generally be placed subject to being hit by only a combination throw.

When providing builders in the outer table, blot on the 11 rather than on the 10, and on the 10 rather than on the 9. The more distant the blot is from the 1-point, the harder it is to hit—and also, the easier it is to use in making the bar- and 5-points.

With the strategic points established, and with no men prematurely moved up into the inner table, and out of play, a position is obtained which permits free and effective action to meet the subsequent changes in the game.

THE DOUBLING GAME

This is played as follows.

An agreed unit is staked upon the game. At any time during the play, when either player considers that he has attained a position of advantage, he may, after his opponent has completed his move and prior to throwing his own dice, double the initial stake. If the opponent thinks his chance of possible success too slight, he refuses, forfeits the original stake, and the game stops. Should he think that his disadvantage may be only temporary—and, in this game, one lucky throw may completely change the out-look—he accepts the double, and the game proceeds. The option of *redoubling* rests with the player who has last been doubled; the original doubler, no matter how much his advantage may have in-creased, may not again, successively raise the stake. Thus the player who is at a temporary disadvantage cannot be "raised out"; he can at least play the game out, and have a run for his money, at no greater expense than he has already assumed. Should the luck shift, however, to the side of the player who was doubled, he, in his turn, may now redouble, quadrupling the original stake. The opponent must now either accept or forfeit the doubled stake. And so it goes; as one side or the other obtains the advantage, the stake increases arithmetically, theoretically indefinitely, but actually it is rare to see more than five or six doubles.

Nevertheless, while the stake may, and does, increase so long as fortune hangs in the balance, a player always knows that, if luck fails, he can carry on to a conclusion with a maximum risk of only twice what he has already staked,— or, indeed, at no further risk, if his opponent was the last to double. This feature uniquely protects the unfortunate.

THE DOUBLING GAME

Thus, the quiet, historic old game, which Dean Swift once termed "the only game a clergyman can consistently play," has been equipped with a variation which has had a sudden, and apparently irresistible appeal to that large class who are habitual seekers after "action."

But this variation has added something beside "action" to the game itself. Just as Contract has required from Auction players a more exact analysis of the possibilities of the hand, so the Doubling Game has emphasized to the Backgammon player the vital importance of ability, at all times, to correctly appraise the relative positions of the opposing sides. In fact, there has been added a new technique, which seems certainly to be the conclusive test of personal skill at the game—ability in the treatment of the Double.

The opening moves are indicated within a small margin of choice, it is demonstrable that variation beyond that margin will be disadvantageous in the long run; subsequent tactics have a reliable basic guide in the consideration of the odds about the possible succeeding throws; the safest method of end play may be comprised in a few simple rules. Therefore, by having in mind the opening formulae, the odds against the various throws, and common-sense precaution in throwing off, a player may evince a mechanical execution which it would be difficult to criticize at any given point—and yet, if he lacks judgment in his treatment of doubling, his game will be but vanity and vexation of spirit when the score is settled.

Effective doubling requires a little psychology and an appreciation of timing, as well as ability to gauge relative position correctly. There comes a time when the player's advantage should be capitalized by a double, but if he delays, say, merely one throw, he may be so far ahead that the doubler will decline. He may suddenly leap into the lead so decisively that it would be folly to offer a double, which no sensible opponent would accept, instead of trying for a double game. Frequently, in a close finish, a thoughtless player, slightly ahead, neglects to end the game by a double, only to see it lost to one or two good throws by an opponent, who would never have paid extra for his lucky long chance.

There is also the psychologically timed double which a timid opponent is daunted from accepting, when he really had a reasonable chance; or the one that a dogged loser will snap at, although there is hardly a ray of hope.

There is only one quality at Backgammon more desirable than judgment in doubling, and that is, judgment in declining a double. Lacking statistics, a fair guess would be, that five times more is lost by unsound acceptance than should be gained by sound offering.

BACKGAMMON OF TODAY

Unsound acceptances seem to spring from a combination of poor judgment and hurt feelings. Many players seem to think that a double is a challenge to their physical courage. Again, there is a large class who will fight their luck to the bitter end, encouraged by some hazy idea about "gameness." Then there are the players, who will never drop a pair of deuces when a jack pot is opened, who realize that the odds are desperately against them, but who will always contribute on the chance of seeing a miracle. And, of course, one of the great fascinations of the game is, that the miracle sometimes happens. In fact, where a pair of dice are the final dispensers of fortune, rules of play based on mathematical probability are constantly triumphantly flouted.

WHEN SHOULD A DOUBLE BE OFFERED?

A rash double is simply putting a weapon into the adversary's hands, so the doubler should be satisfactorily ahead. For instance, the player should double if, early in the game, he has been able to establish two of the three major points (the bar-, 5-, and opponent's 5-) before the adversary has obtained a compensating advantage. In an otherwise even game, if the opponent has a man on the bar and has failed to enter, the player should double; the loss of one throw is a bad setback. An unfortunate throw, compelling the adversary to leave blots which should be easy to hit, frequently offers a sporting opportunity, with the probability of being redoubled, if the hit is not made.

The player should always double when he is well ahead, and there seems no longer a chance for a double game. There is everything to lose and nothing to gain in prolonging the play in this situation, and if the opponent abandons the battle, so much the better. It would be inexcusable to give him the chance for some extraordinary throws without making him pay for them. When throwing off, with a lead of half a throw,* and with men equally placed in the board, or with lower-placed men and the throw even, doubling is advisable. It is true, the lead is slight, but it should last.

WHEN SHOULD A DOUBLE BE ACCEPTED?

Early in the game, or not at all—provided the double is based on an indisputably advantageous position. Twenty yards handicap in a half-mile race may be overcome; in the hundred, it is hopeless. Of course, it does not follow, if the necessary shot is a 17-1 chance, that it *must* be preceded by sixteen failures,—it may occur at once. But the field of opportunity for the unusual lessens steadily as the game draws to an end.

---

* When both are throwing off, and it is Black's throw, if White has already removed five men, and Black four, Black is one-half a throw ahead of White, because, when he has made his throw, he will probably be able to remove two men, and he will then have thrown off six. In like manner, if, prior to Black's throw, both had removed five men each, Black would be a full throw ahead of White, because he could expect to remove two men with his throw.

THE DOUBLING GAME

Some players accept an unfavorable double on the theory that they are thereby obtaining attractive odds. That is, if Black doubles, White's original stake is forfeited unless he accepts. But, by putting up an additional stake, he has a chance to win Black's two, plus the one he has already lost. Therefore he is now getting odds of 3-1. Ingenious but fallacious. White can win nothing unless he puts up an extra stake, in which case he has a chance to win two from Black. But he still stands to lose his original stake, and to win nothing more. He will now either win two, or lose two. He has merely doubled his liability on a disadvantageous proposition. In other words, instead of taking the odds, he has paid, with an even-money bet, to keep alive an odds-against chance.

The only valid reason for laying the odds, which is what this amounts to, lies in the fact that, *if* the lead is regained, the odds on winning at once become greater than the actual mathematical chance, because, if redoubled, the opponent is in turn confronted with the consideration of lessened opportunity, and will resign a certain proportion of games which, if finished, he would have won.

On the other hand, many doubles are based on an apparent advantage which, on analysis, lessens or disappears. The ability to assign to progress and position their correct relative values can only be acquired by experience, but it is an invaluable aid in this situation. For instance, the doubler certainly *thinks* his advantage considerable—but is it? The fact that he has ten men home, against four, may be competely offset by the hazardous position of his outside men. His men may be far ahead in progress, but, if they are so placed that exposures are probable, the advantage of such a lead may be heavily discounted. There are many advantageous positions which need only a few good throws to be impregnable, but are only one *bad* throw from vulnerability. How many of these bad throws are possible? And are men in a position to take advantage of them?

Therefore, while doubling has undoubtedly provided a unique attraction to the game, it has also, and desirably, tremendously emphasized the value of skilful analysis.

RUNNING FOR HOME

While, at the beginning of the game, it is most desirable to combine forward play with hindrance of the opponent's progress, the time arrives when blocking becomes much less important than speeding home. Nice judgment is seldom seen so profitably employed as when choosing the right opportunity to make a run of it. Countless games have been narrowly lost by delaying the start just one or two all-important throws. Remember that this game is not static; what were good tactics at one stage will defeat you if maintained too long. When the adversary's men have got by, and there is little reasonable chance of a hit, the bar- and 8-points have passed their period of usefulness; use the short throws to get them into the board, without delay. A point in the opponent's outer table which did good service in hindering

the adversary loses value steadily as his
men are carried past, and while breaking
it may expose a blot, it may well be that
this risk is the only chance to make the
timely progress which will win the game.
(See diagram 15.)

Here is a typical situation. Black is one
average throw—8 points—ahead. Suppose he throws 5-3. A superficial player
would make the point in the board,
reasoning, first, that he was playing
"safe," and further, that if he should
happen to hit one of White's back men,
White would have little more than an
even chance to enter, and might lose a
throw. And both these thoughts are
correct; but examine the position more
closely. In the first place, it is unlikely
that White will have to expose a blot,
because he has the larger number of men
outside, with which to take care of
inconveniently long throws, therefore
Black will probably be the one eventually
compelled to "break." Again, if Black

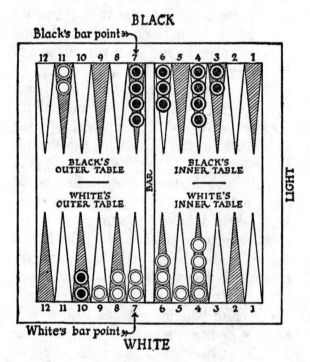

Diagram 15

is determined to play "safe," he will have to wait until he throws either double 3's, 5's, 6's or 6-5, for which he has less than one chance in six; meanwhile White can use all his throws to full advantage, in completing a formidable board, and in evening up his slight disadvantage in progress.

Black's best move is to play one of the men on White's 10 to his own 10, and the other to his own 12. This gets one man safe, and with the other he is only blotting against exactly a 1, with odds of 3-2 against being hit. If he is not hit, he has a winning lead; if he is hit, he will have a great deal better chance with White's board now, than later.

When running, be careful to use every pip on your dice to bring your men over your bar with the least waste. Diagram 16 illustrates a position showing the desirability of economy of movement.

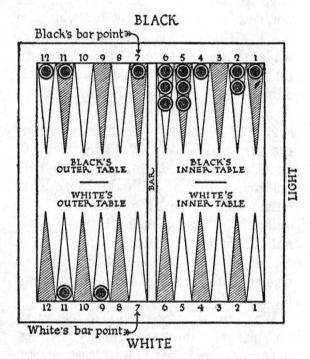

Diagram 16

RUNNING FOR HOME

Here, if Black throws a 4, he should bring the man on White's 9-point over to his own 12, so that it can cross the bar with the throw of a single die. In like manner, a 2 should bring the man on White's 11 to Black's 12,—it should *not* bring home the man on the bar-point. It would be a waste of ammunition to use a 6 to carry the man on the 11- instead of the man on the 12-point.

While men are still outside, do not use throws to move the men inside further into the table. It is true that men on the low points come off quicker, if small dice are thrown; it is equally true that no men at all come off until they are all across the bar. It is a commonly held, but fallacious, belief that the player who carries his men deep into the board, and then begins to throw off, will fare better than, or, at least, as well as, the player who, with identical throws, gets his men barely over the bar, and thereby begins to bear them earlier. It is mathematically demonstrable that, on the average (not every time) with identical throws, the player who *first gets his men in* will be first to bear them off.

THROWING OFF

When the inner table is free of opposing men, throwing off is a simple matter. Use every pip of the throw to *get the men off*. For instance, with all remaining men on the 5- and 6-points, and a throw of, say, 4-2 or 3-2, bear one man; do not play down in the board, to take advantage of a subsequent low throw; such a throw may never be made, and this play sacrifices the substance for the shadow. With the men grouped on three or four points, use any throw, which does not bear a man, to fill the vacant points, if possible.

Play must be carefully planned, however, if a point in the board is occupied by the adversary. Foresight is possible here—since the point will have been held before all men are home—and should be used. Suppose, first (which is less frequent), that it is one of the higher

points, the 3- or 4-. Be especially careful
for the safety of the outside men which
have still to reach home. If a blot must
be left, select one vulnerable only to
double dice. The 6- and 5-points in the
board are extremely valuable as stepping
stones for outside men; but even these
should be abandoned rather than leave a
blot, at this stage, which can be hit by a
single die. (See diagram 17.)

Black has thrown 5-4. He can play
safe by breaking up his 6-point, but it
would be ill-advised since this would
greatly increase the difficulty for the outside men. One of the men on the 12-
should be brought home. This is blotting against a 6-2 or 5-3 (double-4 will
not play), an 8-1 chance, and, if not hit,
it is 5-1 in favor of safety on the next
throw, for the only bad shots are 2-1,
3-2 and 5-3.

Suppose, however, that the two men
on the 12- are home, and only the two
men on the 8- are outside when this

THROWING OFF

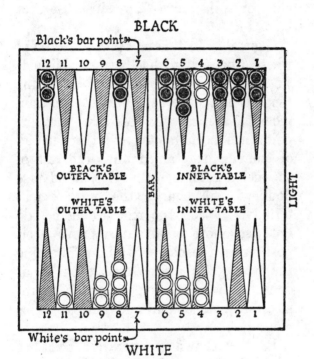

Diagram 17

throw is made. Then the 6-point must go; for it is only 3-2 against the blot being hit.

Generally, in this end position (except where a back game has been established) we find the two opposing men on the 1-point, as the result of earlier successful blocking tactics. In this case, the bar-point has been made, and this should, of course, be retained until the rest of the men are home; otherwise, an adverse double-6 will change the outlook materially. When the rest are home, do not use short shots to improve their position in the board, while maintaining the bar; get the men on the bar in at once. Otherwise, the position is jeopardized for an inadequate advantage. (See diagram 18.)

Here is shown comparative positions where both sides have all men in the board, but Black has delayed breaking his bar point until his men have moved up in his table. The X's represent

THROWING OFF

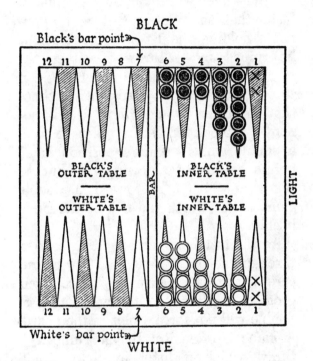

Black's bar point

12 11 10 9 8 7 6 5 4 3 2 1

BLACK'S
OUTER TABLE

BLACK'S
INNER TABLE

BAR

LIGHT

WHITE'S
OUTER TABLE

WHITE'S
INNER TABLE

12 11 10 9 8 7 6 5 4 3 2 1

White's bar point

WHITE

Diagram 18

potential opponents. With even throws, the Black men will undoubtedly come off faster than the White. But, with opponents holding the 1-point, Black might be ruined by a throw of either 6-5 or 5-4. White, on the other hand, can throw off in safety so many times that prudence would impel the opponent to break early, in order to save a double game. Black's position is 17 points better for throwing off, but so slight an advantage toward a double game is not worth the risk of the game itself.

As the last few men are being carried through the outer table into the board, care should be taken to space their progress so that the throw of a large double will not force a blot in the board. A game is often lost by an "unlucky" throw which a little foresight would have rendered innocuous.

Here is a position which appears not infrequently: (See diagram 19.)

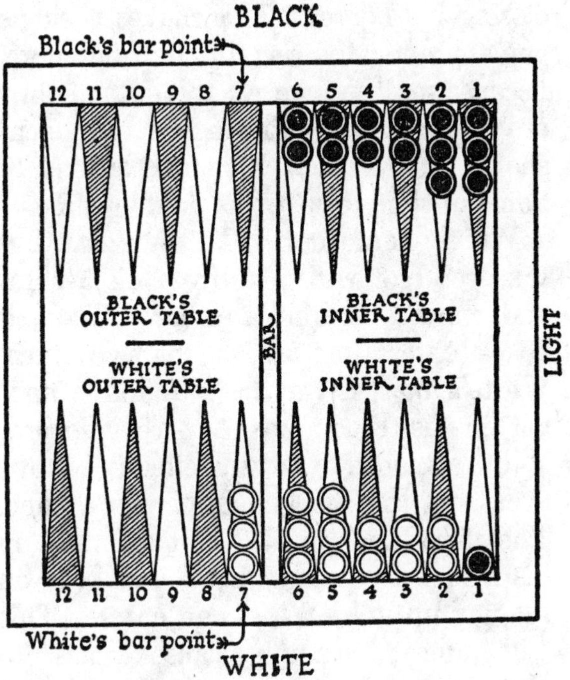
BLACK
Black's bar point
12 11 10 9 8 7 6 5 4 3 2 1
BLACK'S OUTER TABLE
WHITE'S OUTER TABLE
BAR
BLACK'S INNER TABLE
WHITE'S INNER TABLE
LIGHT
12 11 10 9 8 7 6 5 4 3 2 1
White's bar point
WHITE

Diagram 19

White has thrown 5-4. He can, of course, hit the blot and make a point, closing his board. This makes a single game practically certain, but no more, because, as the men on the outer points are thrown off, the single opponent should easily enter and move around to home in time to save the double game.

White should not make the point, but take the blot with a 4, from his 5-point and move 5 in from the bar. Then, if Black enters, hitting the blot, in turn, White's man is on the bar and cannot get in, as Black has a perfect board. White's blockade is still effective, however, and the Black man cannot escape. Therefore Black must begin to break up his board on his next shot, and keep on moving up until White can enter. This will almost certainly cause Black to blot, and if White hits the blot in re-entering, he has an excellent chance for a double game. The two Black men cannot get away, and will eventually be taken up, as White moves in. They cannot re-enter until White has cleared his 6-point, and six average shots would be necessary (more, unless they entered at once) to enter and get both men home. Meanwhile, White, bearing two men with each shot, should have thrown off all his men.

Note that this method of play does not jeopardize the single game, for if White does not hit a man, on re-entering, he can move around at his leisure, since his blockade is always effective.

CHOUETTE

This is a method of play, not confined to Backgammon—originally it was used at Piquet,—by which a game, primarily for two, may be played by several. The French Chouette, or screech owl, is always attacked by all the other birds; therefore, here, one player, who is "in the box," is opposed by all the others.

Each player throws one die. The highest number is "in the box," the next highest becomes his playing opponent, and the other allies back the play of this opponent with their stake, and, if he is defeated, succeed to his position in the order of their dice.

The "box" therefore risks as many times the agreed stake as there are players against him. But he plays this multiple stake only while winning; as soon as he loses a game, he takes his place as the last of the allies, the winning opponent takes the "box," and is in turn played by the next succeeding ally. Thus, while success is profitable to the player in the "box," ill luck is not disastrous, because he can lose only one game at multiple stakes.

The game itself is played as usual: doubles, redoubles, and double games increasing the initial stake in the customary manner, for each player. The only original feature is in the relationship between the allies and their playing representative. Each move is subject to the discussion, criticism, and suggestion of any of them, but the final decision rests with the actual player, and, in regard to the play his action is binding on all his associates. Any increase of the stake, however, is a matter of individual option. No one is compelled to offer or accept a double which he considers disadvantageous.

For instance, A is playing in the "box" against B, C, D, and E. A doubles, thereby offering to play for eight times the stake. *B* and *C* are willing to accept the double, but *D* and *E* consider the position unfavorable. *D* and *E* then forfeit their original stakes to *B* and *C*, and their interest in that game is terminated. *B* and *C* then jointly put up the eight stakes called for by *A's* double, and the game proceeds, with *B* and *C* sharing the final profit or loss.

In like manner, should *B*, who is playing, wish to double but *C*, *D* and *E* disapprove, the three latter forfeit their original stakes to *B*, who thenceforward assumes all financial liability for the game.

NOTES ON PLAY

The Cardinal Sin is to crowd men deep in the inner table early in the game. It is the only bad play that cannot be redeemed. This situation generally arises either from timidity in exposing blots, or a false idea of the value of the lower points. (See diagram 20.)

Here, White played first, and threw 5-3, 6-4 and double-5. Black threw the same throws in the same sequence. The disproportionate number of White's men which have been immediately put out of play, without adequate compensation, and which he can never remobilize, puts him at a serious disadvantage.

While it is true that each man hit delays the adversary's progress, this can easily be overdone, in the early part of the game. After one man has been taken, putting three in the inner table,

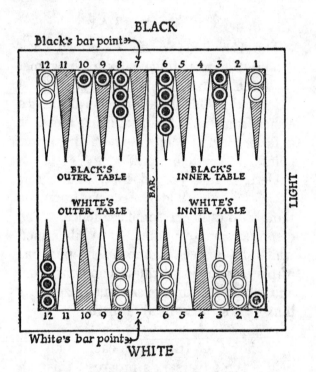

Diagram 20

the desirability of adding to that number—unless a point can be made in the
board—is doubtful. It is a common,
and serious mistake to use a shot which
could materially improve the position
of the outside men, to gather up additional blots. With a number of men
early on the bar, the opponent may
easily establish a good back game. If
four men are hit, two adverse points in
the table are a serious threat to the
homecoming men. The necessity for
this precaution disappears, of course, as
the game progresses, and points are
made in the board, and the adversary's
men are so far advanced that a back
game would be out of timing.

One of the commonest faults of medi-
ocre play is the careless waste of throws
when bringing men home. Games are
constantly, and needlessly, lost by the
failure to realize how important it is to
place the incoming men so that it may be

possible to carry them into the inner table, or throw them off, with a *single die*. There is the difference of half a throw between the opponent's 12-point and the player's 12-point, or between the bar and the 6-point. To use every pip thrown to carry a man *just* into the outer table, or *just* over the bar, is a rigid economy of available resources which brings gratifying returns. Not invariably, however, because the necessary single die *may* not be thrown; but, if the man is not in position to take advantage of it, it *cannot* be thrown.

When running, the first essential is to get all of the men *over the bar* in the fewest number of throws.

Unless shots like doublets, or 6-5's make it practically compulsory, it is inadvisable to move *both* men away from the opponent's 1-point. Let one man go at any favorable opportunity, but the nuisance value of one man, all the

way back, is enormous, and diminishes
to nothing, as the man is moved forward
in the table.

––––––––

With men scattered, and a throw
which entails a blot, or blots, the play
should be made only after carefully
reckoning the damaging throws, and
their comparative probability, that the
adversary can make. This reckoning
should include doublets; they occur infrequently, but, if not allowed for, they
may be disastrous.

––––––––

Here is a situation which frequently
occurs, with the exact positions some-
what changed, but presenting the same
problem: (See diagram 21.)

Black has thrown 6-4. He can move
the outside man 4, then 6, and should
be able to get all his men in before the
White man can make the trip home.
But White has so much better board

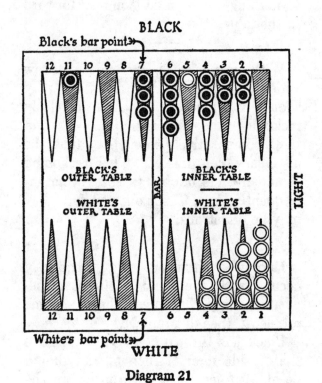

Diagram 21

that, without greatly superior throws, Black must lose.

Black's play, therefore, should be, 6-4, hitting the White man and leaving a blot on his 1-point. He *must* gain a throw or two, and this is his only way to do it. With four points held, White has a 5-4 chance of immediate re-entry. There is a fair possibility that a throw may be gained here. If the man enters on the 5, only one die can be used for progress, and half a throw is gained. If White enters on the 1, hitting the blot, Black then has a 5-4 prospect of immediate entry, and should get back home in two more shots. White, on the other hand, to escape, must throw exactly double-4, 4-3, 4-5 or 4-6, for which he has slightly less than one chance in four, and then must still get home, before beginning to throw off. There is now a strong probability that Black will gain the necessary throws—at all events, this method of play gives him his best chance.

BACKGAMMON OF TODAY

Finally, and to repeat, if a man must be exposed, blot against a combination shot, or, if this is not possible, place the blot as near as may be to the threatening adversary.

FOREWORD TO THE RULES

Interest in the game of Backgammon is widespread, and is increasing daily. It is clearly most desirable that a standard method of play should be understood and adopted. There are at present in existence no adequate printed rules for the game, as it is now played.

The rules given herewith have been submitted to, and approved by, the clubs where the game has been longest played, and where the modern variations have been developed.

In some of the present rules, optional alternatives have been given, to cover certain minor differences in local procedure.

It is hoped that, as the game becomes more generally played, arrangement can be made for a committee composed of delegates from the clubs interested, which will promulgate an official code. Meanwhile, the rules, as here given, represent a consensus of the opinion of the best available authorities.

THE RULES OF BACKGAMMON

SPECIFICALLY APPROVED BY
THE CLUBS IN WHICH THE PRESENT-DAY GAME
ORIGINATED AND WAS DEVELOPED

1. The game may be played with either; (*a*) Two dice boxes and two sets of dice; (*b*) Two dice boxes and one set of dice; (*c*) One dice box and one set of dice. The player throwing the highest die shall have the choice, in case of disagreement.

2. The men are set up so that the inner tables shall be nearest the light. Decision of position of light and choice of men

shall be made by the player throwing the highest single die.

3. If, at any time during the game it is discovered that the men have been wrongly set up, play ceases, and that game is void.

4. For the first move; (a) Each player throws a single die; he who throws the higher number wins, and, for his first move, plays the pips on both his own and his opponent's die. After that, each player throws and plays two dice, (b) Each player throws two dice; he who throws the highest number wins, and for his first move may either play the throw he has already made, or throw again, in which case, the second throw *must* be played.

5. Each tie, when throwing for first move, automatically doubles the stake.

NOTE: By mutual agreement, before play has begun, automatic doubles may be limited in number, or need not be played.

6. Both dice must be taken up and thrown again:

    (*a*) If the player has not thrown the dice into the tables on his right hand.

    (*b*) If either die is upon, or "cocked" against, the other die, a man, or the side or end of the tables.

    (*c*) If either die jumps into the other tables or off the board.

    (*d*) If either player touches either die after it has been thrown, and before it has come to rest.

7. The player must leave his dice upon the board until his play is completed. Should he pick them up before the completion of his play, the opponent may, at his option, declare the play void, and require the offender to replace the man or men moved, and to throw again.

8. A play is completed when the move or moves required by the dice have been made, and the man or men quitted.

After a play has been so completed, it cannot be changed.

9. If a man has been moved the wrong number of points, or entered incorrectly, or thrown off before all are home, the opponent may, at his option, and before he has thrown, demand that the error be corrected. After the opponent has thrown, errors of play cannot be corrected except by mutual consent.

10. The numbers on both dice must be played if possible. Either may be played first. If either, but only one, of the numbers thrown can be played, the higher must be played.

11. Whenever a man has been moved from its position upon a point it must be played if possible.

12. If a player throw his dice before his adversary's throw is completed, the throw is void, and he must throw again.

13. CHOUETTE: In play against the Box, the decision of the Player is binding

upon his Associates, in a question of play. In a question of doubling, redoubling, or acceptance of a double, the decision of the Player is final, but any associate, disagreeing, may terminate his interest in that game by forfeiting his stake already at risk to the Associates who continue to play. Thereafter all liability for, or profit from, the interest so resigned, is shared equally by the continuing Associates.

14. (a) A Single game is won by the player first to throw off all of his men.

   (b) A Double game, or "Gammon," is won if the player has thrown off all of his men before the adversary has thrown off any man.

   (c) A Triple game, or "Backgammon," is won if the player has thrown off all of his men before the adversary

THE RULES OF BACKGAMMON

has thrown off any man, and has not carried all of his men out of the winner's inner table.

NOTE: By mutual agreement, before play has begun, Triple games need not be played.

DEFINITION OF TERMS

Bar. The raised partition dividing the board.

Bar, "on the." Taken up; when a man has been hit, he is placed on the bar, awaiting re-entry.

Bar Point. The point in the outer table, nearest to the bar.

Bear. To remove a man from the inner table, according to the dice thrown; to throw off.

Block, Blockade. To establish points which prevent the movement of opposing men.

Blot. An exposed single man; a single man is always subject to being hit by the adversary.

Carry. To move a man.

Doublets. Two dice with the same number of pips. Four times the number of the pips on one die is available for moving the men.

Enter, Re-enter. To place a man who has been "on the bar" on a point in the opponent's inner table.

Game, Single, is won by the player first to throw off all of his men; **Double, or Gammon,** is won if the player has thrown off all his men before his opponent has thrown off any man; **Triple,** or **Backgammon,** is won if the player has thrown off all his men before the opponent has thrown off any man and before he has carried all of his men out of the winner's inner table.

Half-Throw. In throwing off, the player about to throw, who has removed one more man than his opponent, is said to be a half-throw ahead.

Hit. When a man can be moved exactly to the point occupied by a single opponent, that opponent is hit and is taken up and placed on the bar.

Pips. The spots on the dice.

Point. (a) One of the twenty-four long, triangular spaces on the board.

(b) "to make a." To establish two or more men on a point. Opposing men can not rest on a point so made.

Position. The location of the men.

Progress. The movement of the men towards and into the inner table, and their removal therefrom.

Side Prime. A blockade of six consecutive points.

Table. One-fourth of the board. **Inner Table** is that quarter into which the men are moved and from which they are thrown off. **Outer Table** is the quarter immediately adjacent, across the bar, on the same side of the board.

Take Up. To hit.

Throw Off. To bear; to remove from the inner table.